TIMELINES

The Cold War

R. G. Grant

ARCTURUS

This edition first published by Arcturus Publishing
Distributed by Black Rabbit Books
123 South Broad Street
Mankato
Minnesota MN 56001

Library of Congress Cataloging-in-Publication Data
Grant, Reg, 1954-
  The Cold War / by Reg Grant.
      p. cm. -- (Timelines)
Includes bibliographical references and index.
ISBN 978-1-84193-726-7 (alk. paper)
1. Cold War--Juvenile literature.
2. Cold War--Chronology--Juvenile literature. I. Title. II. Series.

D1058.G626 2007
909.82'5--dc22

                  2007007548

9 8 7 6 5 4 3 2

Series concept: Alex Woolf
Project manager and editor: Helen Maxey
Designer: Simon Borrough
Picture researcher: Helen Maxey
Consultant: James Vaughan

Contents

Yalta Conference

In February 1945, U.S. president Franklin D. Roosevelt, British prime minister Winston Churchill and Joseph Stalin, dictator of the Soviet Union, met at Yalta, in the Crimea. Known as the Big Three, these men were allies in a war against Nazi Germany, which they were close to winning.

The Big Three had built up a good working relationship during the war but there were deep divisions buried under the surface. Created by the Russian Revolution of 1917, the Soviet Union was the world's first Communist state and was committed, in theory, to the overthrow of global capitalism. Stalin was a dictator, ruling his country through a secret police. Millions of Soviet citizens had been sent to prison camps for allegedly opposing Stalin's regime. Roosevelt and Churchill, by contrast, were committed to the principles of individual freedom, democracy, and a capitalist free-market economy.

OCCUPATION OF GERMANY

Although the Western Allies and the Soviets did not fully trust one another, the Yalta meeting was on the whole harmonious and good-humored. The leaders agreed that when they had defeated Germany they would divide it into zones of military occupation, with the Soviet Union taking the eastern zone. Stalin also agreed that after Germany's defeat he would join in the war the U.S. and Britain were fighting against Japan. To please the Western Allies,

Divided Europe

At the end of the fighting with Germany in 1945, the Soviet army controlled what became known as Eastern Europe—Poland, Czechoslovakia, Hungary, Bulgaria, Romania, and Yugoslavia, plus the eastern parts of Germany and Austria. Except for eastern Austria, all the territories occupied by Soviet forces at the war's end finished up with Communist governments, although Yugoslavia became fully independent of the Soviet Union.

The Big Three meet at Yalta: left to right, Winston Churchill, Franklin D. Roosevelt, and Joseph Stalin. Roosevelt died two months later.

TIMELINE

he promised to hold democratic elections in Poland, liberated from German control by the victorious Soviet army. This was a promise he did not intend to keep.

By the following July, when the leaders of Britain, the U.S., and the Soviet Union met at Potsdam in Germany, Germany had been defeated and Roosevelt had died, replaced as president by Harry S. Truman. During the Potsdam conference, Churchill was also replaced as prime minister by Clement Attlee, after losing a general election.

POSTWAR COOPERATION

Truman had a more confrontational attitude to Stalin than Roosevelt but, nonetheless, arrangements for the occupation of Germany were implemented as agreed. There was still a general belief that the Allies, despite their differences, would continue to cooperate in the postwar world.

A Red Army soldier raises the flag of the Soviet Union in Berlin as Stalin's forces occupy the German capital in spring 1945.

**CROSS-REFERENCE
THE IRON CURTAIN:
PAGES 6–7
OCCUPIED
GERMANY:
PAGES 8–9**

Truman Doctrine Proclaimed

President Harry S. Truman, left, meets with foreign policy advisers in the White House in 1946.

On March 12, 1947, U.S. President Harry S. Truman made an urgent foreign policy statement to a joint session of Congress. Announcing that the U.S. was giving aid to the governments of Greece and Turkey, the president more broadly committed his country to containing Communism worldwide—that is, preventing new Communist governments coming to power outside the area controlled by the Soviet Union at the end of World War II. This became known as the Truman Doctrine.

Soviet expansionism

The U.S. government's new stance reflected a changing perception of the Soviet Union. Truman and his advisers had become convinced that Stalin was bent on expanding Soviet control over an ever-wider area, either through military aggression or by encouraging Communist seizure of power using guerrilla warfare or other non-democratic means.

"Iron Curtain" speech

"From Stettin in the Baltic to Trieste in the Adriatic, **an iron curtain has descended** across the Continent. Behind that line . . . all are subject, in one form or another, not only to Soviet influence but to a very high and in some cases increasing measure of control from Moscow. . . . I do not believe that Soviet Russia desires war. What they desire is the fruits of war and the indefinite expansion of their power and doctrines."

From Winston Churchill's famous "Iron Curtain" speech, given in Fulton, Missouri, March 5, 1946.

In his speech, Truman claimed that the U.S. would be supporting "free peoples" against "subjugation" (control) by Communists. This claim seemed reasonable, given events in Soviet-controlled Eastern Europe, where a Stalinist system was imposed on every country by 1948. This meant that all power was concentrated in the hands of a Communist Party, and a secret police was used to crush dissent. Nonetheless, Communist parties enjoyed a large degree of popular support in some West European countries, especially Italy.

THE MARSHALL PLAN

Three months after Truman's statement, U.S. Secretary of State George Marshall proposed massive financial aid to rebuild Europe. The Marshall Plan was based on the calculation that economic recovery would draw Europeans away from supporting Communism and make Western Europe strong enough to resist Soviet expansionism. The aid was also offered to Eastern Europe but Stalin refused to accept it, correctly judging that the money would come with restrictive conditions. When West European Communist parties, under Stalin's orders, opposed acceptance of Marshall aid, their chances of electoral success slumped.

CROSS-REFERENCE
NATO FORMED: PAGES 8–9
RESISTING COMMUNISM IN KOREA: PAGES 12–13

Italian Communists march with banners in 1949. The U.S. feared that Communist parties might win power in West European countries.

Soviets Impose Berlin Blockade

At the end of World War II, defeated Germany was divided into four zones. These were occupied respectively by the forces of the U.S., Britain, France, and the Soviet Union. The former German capital, Berlin, lay deep inside the Soviet occupation zone but it was also divided between U.S., British, French, and Soviet forces, with each running their own sector of the city.

The wartime Allies were supposed to cooperate in running Germany through a joint Allied Control Council but they couldn't reach any agreement on the country's future. By March 1948, the U.S., Britain, and France were openly planning to set up a democratic German government in the three zones they controlled. Angered by this, the Soviet Union withdrew from the Allied Control Council.

Plunging on regardless, in June 1948, the Western Allies introduced a new currency in their three zones. On June 24, in protest at the currency reform, the Soviet Union cut all road and rail links between the Western occupation zones and Berlin. The Western Allies appeared to be faced with a choice between agreeing to pull their forces out of their sectors of Berlin—known as West Berlin—or abandoning the currency reform. The inhabitants of West Berlin were clear that they did not want to be handed over to Communist control.

DEFEATING THE SOVIETS

Initially with little hope of success, the U.S. and Britain embarked on an airlift, attempting to supply the 2.5 million people of West Berlin with food and fuel by air. Transport aircraft used air corridors that the Soviet Union, not wanting to provoke a war, did not attempt to block. At the cost of 54 airmen's lives, they succeeded in keeping West Berlin supplied through a severe winter. By the following spring, the Soviet Union was forced to admit defeat and lift the blockade.

West Berliners wave at one of the Allied transport aircraft that keep them supplied with fuel and food during the Berlin blockade.

TIMELINE

DISPUTE OVER
GERMANY
1945–1955

July 3, 1945	Soviet Union allows British, U.S., and French troops to occupy sectors of Berlin.
August 30, 1945	Allied Control Council is formed to govern Germany, which is divided into occupation zones.
March 20, 1948	Soviet Union walks out of Allied Control Council.
June 20, 1948	Britain, U.S., and France launch new currency in their occupation zones.
June 24, 1948	Berlin blockade begins.
April 4, 1949	NATO is founded.
May 12, 1949	End of the Berlin blockade.
May 23, 1949	British, French, and U.S. zones of Germany become Federal Republic of Germany.
October 7, 1949	Soviet occupation zone becomes German Democratic Republic.
May 9, 1955	West Germany joins NATO.
May 14, 1955	Warsaw Pact is founded.

The confrontation over Berlin cemented the Cold War division of Europe. The Western Allies created the Federal Republic of Germany, or West Germany, under democratic government, while the Soviet Union turned its occupation zone into the Communist-ruled German Democratic Republic. Before the blockade ended, the U.S. had committed itself to the military defense of Western Europe through the NATO alliance, which West Germany would eventually join. Berlin remained a divided city, occupied by U.S., French, British, and Soviet forces.

President Truman signs the pact creating NATO, the alliance that tied the U.S. to the defense of Western Europe.

CROSS-REFERENCE
BUILDING OF
BERLIN WALL:
PAGES 24–25

NATO and the Warsaw Pact

The founder members of NATO in 1949 were: Belgium, Canada, Denmark, France, Iceland, Italy, Luxembourg, Netherlands, Norway, Portugal, the United Kingdom, and the U.S. Greece and Turkey joined NATO in 1952, and West Germany joined in 1955.

Founder members of the Warsaw Pact in 1955 were Albania, Bulgaria, Czechoslovakia, Hungary, Poland, and Romania. East Germany joined in 1956; Albania withdrew in 1962.

Communists Take Power in China

The civil war between the Nationalist government of China, headed by Chiang Kai-shek, and Chinese Communist guerrillas, led by Mao Zedong, began in 1927. When Japan invaded China in 1937, the Nationalists and Communists formed an alliance against the invaders. However, after the Japanese surrendered in August 1945, defeated by the Allies, the civil war in China soon resumed.

The Soviet Union, which occupied Manchuria in northern China at the end of World War II, helped the Chinese Communists establish a strong position there. But Stalin did not encourage Mao to try to take power in China, suggesting instead that he reach an agreement with Chiang Kai-shek. The U.S., while supplying the Nationalists with money and arms, also tried to push the two sides into making a compromise agreement. A ceasefire arranged by the Americans in January 1946 soon broke down, however, and the scale of the fighting continued to grow.

The Chinese Communists succeeded in winning a great deal of popular support in rural areas they controlled, through a reform programme that gave land to peasants. The Nationalists, by contrast, were notoriously corrupt and failed to stop runaway inflation. Their soldiers became increasingly disillusioned and began to desert in large numbers. In the summer of 1949, Chiang took refuge with the remnants of his armies on the island of Formosa (Taiwan). The Communists occupied Beijing and Mao declared China a People's Republic.

Mao Zedong proclaims the founding of the People's Republic of China in Tiananmen Square on October 1, 1949.

ALLIANCE WITH STALIN

The U.S. government was not prepared to undertake the major war that would have been required to challenge Communist power in China. Instead, there were hopes that a deal could be struck with Mao, to stop

CHINA—CIVIL WAR TO KOREAN WAR 1945–1950

August 8, 1945	▶ Soviet troops invade Japanese-occupied Manchuria after the Soviet Union declares war on Japan.
October 1945	▶ Chinese Nationalists and Communists begin fight for control of Manchuria.
January 10, 1946	▶ Nationalists and Communists agree ceasefire under pressure from U.S.
July 1946	▶ Nationalists launch major offensive in Manchuria.
January 10, 1949	▶ Communists defeat Nationalists at Xuzhou.
July 1949	▶ Nationalists begin evacuation of forces to Formosa (Taiwan).
October 1, 1949	▶ Mao Zedong proclaims People's Republic of China.
February 1950	▶ Mao negotiates alliance with the Soviet Union.
June 26, 1950	▶ U.S. fleet is sent to protect Nationalist-ruled Formosa from Communist China.
October 1950	▶ Communist Chinese forces enter the Korean War.

China joining the Soviet bloc. But in early 1950, Mao sought an alliance with Stalin. After the outbreak of the Korean War in June 1950, the U.S. gave its support to the Nationalists in Taiwan, refusing to recognize the Chinese Communist government as the legitimate government of China. By the end of 1950, Chinese and U.S. troops were fighting in Korea.

Mao, front left, attends the celebrations for Stalin's birthday in Moscow, April 1950.

CROSS-REFERENCE
KOREAN WAR:
PAGES 12–13
NIXON MEETS MAO:
PAGES 32–33

Allies of the Soviets

"[We must] ally ourselves with the Soviet Union. . . . In the epoch in which imperialism exists it is impossible for a genuine people's revolution to win victory in any country without various forms of **help from international revolutionary forces,** and even if victory were won, it could not be consolidated. . . . Would the present rulers of Britain and the USA, who are imperialists, help a people's state?"

From a speech by Mao Zedong on the "People's Democratic Dictatorship," June 30, 1949.

Korean War Begins

Communist Chinese soldiers are taken prisoner by U.S. Marines during the Korean War.

In June 1950, Communist North Korea launched a full-scale invasion of South Korea, starting a war that would last three years and cost over 5 million lives.

NORTH–SOUTH DIVIDE

At the end of World War II, the Soviet Union and the U.S. had agreed to divide Korea into zones of military occupation, Soviet troops running the northern half and U.S. troops the south. The division was intended to be temporary but, as in Germany, the Soviets and Americans could not agree on a form of government for Korea. Instead, a pro-U.S. government was established in the south and a Soviet-backed government in the north.

When the north invaded the south on June 25, 1950, the U.S. immediately sent forces to aid South Korea, winning the backing of the United Nations (UN) for its military action. Fifteen countries, including Britain,

Deaths in the Korean War

COUNTRY	NO. KILLED (MILITARY)	NO. KILLED (CIVILIAN)
China	1 million*	—
North Korea	500,000*	2 million*
South Korea	415,000*	1 million*
U.S.	33,686	—
Turkey	1,148	—
Britain	1,078	—
Other	2,000*	—
TOTAL	1,954,000*	3 MILLION*

* approximate figures

sent troops to join the U.S.-led UN forces aiding South Korea. By the end of September 1950, UN forces had driven the North Koreans out of South Korea. The commander in Korea, General Douglas MacArthur, then launched an invasion of North Korea. Counter to instructions from the U.S. government, MacArthur advanced up to Korea's border with Communist China. The Chinese then sent troops into North Korea to attack the UN forces and drove them back into South Korea.

For a short time in the winter of 1950–1951, it appeared that the U.S.-led forces might be forced to abandon Korea altogether. President Truman declared a state of emergency in the U.S. and seriously considered using atomic weapons against the Chinese. However, the military situation in Korea soon stabilized. MacArthur was sacked and the war settled into a costly stalemate, lasting another two years. At its end, Korea remained divided.

SHAPING THE FUTURE

The Korean War dramatically affected the development of the Cold War. It led the U.S. to begin a massive arms buildup, ready for any repeat of what it called "Communist aggression." At the same time, it taught America and the Soviet Union the concept of "limited war." Although U.S. and Chinese troops fought one another in Korea, the U.S. did not directly attack China. The Soviet Union backed North Korea but followed strict rules to avoid provoking direct war with the U.S. Although a Third World War never happened, millions more people were destined to die in other "limited wars" of the Cold War period.

CROSS-REFERENCE
VIETNAM WAR:
PAGES 28–29

General Douglas MacArthur, UN commander in Korea, was sacked for ignoring U.S. government instructions to limit the scope of the war.

First H-bomb Test

On November 1, 1952, the U.S. tested the world's first hydrogen bomb (H-bomb) on Elugelab Island in the Pacific Ocean. The explosion totally obliterated the island, leaving a crater about 1.25 miles (2 km) wide. The Americans had succeeded in creating the most powerful weapon ever, and, in the process, dangerously escalated a nuclear arms race with the Soviet Union.

The U.S. had built the first nuclear weapons during World War II and demonstrated their awesome destructive power in August 1945, when atom bombs destroyed the Japanese cities of Hiroshima and Nagasaki. Being the only country with nuclear weapons gave the U.S. a great advantage in the postwar world but the Soviet Union rushed to develop its own atom bombs, helped by information from spies in the West. When the Soviets successfully tested their first nuclear device in August 1949, Americans were shocked and frightened.

THE ARMS RACE TAKES OFF

Both the Americans and the Soviets pressed on with the development of hydrogen bombs, which were far more powerful than atom bombs. The device exploded on Elugelab Island had 450 times the power of the atom bombs dropped on Japan. Both sides in the Cold War also worked on developing delivery systems for

The first H-bomb is tested on Elugelab Island in the Pacific, creating the largest human-made explosion that had ever been seen.

Estimated figures for strategic nuclear weapons, 1961 and 1969

	Intercontinental ballistic missiles (ICBMs)	Submarine-launched ballistic missiles (SLBMs)	Long-range bombers
1961			
U.S.	50	100	600
Soviet Union	0	50	50
1969			
U.S.	1,050	650	560
Soviet Union	1,028	196	145

DEVELOPMENT OF NUCLEAR WEAPONRY 1945–1960

July 16, 1945	▶ First successful test of atomic device is carried out in New Mexico.
August 6, 1945	▶ Hiroshima is destroyed by atomic bomb; Nagasaki is bombed 3 days later.
August 29, 1949	▶ Soviet Union carries out its first atom bomb test.
November 1, 1952	▶ U.S. tests its first hydrogen bomb.
August 12, 1953	▶ Soviet Union explodes a device similar to a hydrogen bomb.
November 22, 1955	▶ Soviet Union tests its first true hydrogen bomb.
August 21, 1957	▶ Soviet Union test launches its first intercontinental ballistic missile (ICBM).
January 10, 1958	▶ First U.S. ICBM is tested.
November 15, 1960	▶ U.S. fires first Polaris missile from a submarine.

nuclear weapons. At first they could only be dropped as bombs from aircraft but in the course of the 1950s, long-range missiles, capable of carrying nuclear warheads, were developed. Elaborate early warning systems were put in place to detect a surprise nuclear attack and trigger a nuclear counterstrike.

U.S. SUPERIORITY

The U.S. maintained clear superiority in nuclear weapons over the Soviet Union into the early 1960s but this was not obvious at the time to the American people or government. The Soviet Union had at least sufficient nuclear weaponry to threaten U.S. cities with destruction. It was assumed that if full-scale war broke out between the two "superpowers," many millions of civilians would die in a few days, or even hours. Neither side would be able to protect its citizens from casualties on a vast scale.

According to the theory of "nuclear deterrence," this mutual threat maintained peace between the superpowers, since neither side could launch a full-scale war without itself suffering massive destruction. It was, however, a dangerous development in world affairs.

A U.S. Atlas missile is readied for launch. Armed with nuclear warheads, such missiles threatened destruction on an unimaginable scale.

CROSS-REFERENCE
CUBAN MISSILE
CRISIS: PAGES
26–27

Rosenbergs Executed for Espionage

Julius and Ethel Rosenberg were an American couple convicted of passing secrets to the Soviet Union. Their trial and subsequent execution in the electric chair aroused intense controversy. Many people felt that the Rosenbergs were innocent victims of a wave of paranoia sweeping the U.S., which had given rise to excessive fears of hidden Communist agents threatening U.S. security. Others felt that, as spies and traitors, they got what they deserved.

One of the first signs of American anxiety about Soviet espionage and Communist subversion had been an investigation of the Hollywood film industry in 1947. Carried out by the U.S. House of Representatives' Un-American Activities Committee (HUAC), it led to the banning of some alleged Communists or Communist sympathizers from working in Hollywood movies. In 1948, a journalist and former Communist, Whittaker Chambers, told HUAC that a senior State Department official, Alger Hiss, had been a Soviet agent. This fueled fears of Communist infiltration of the U.S. government.

MCCARTHYISM

The U.S.'s sense of insecurity reached fever pitch after the Soviet test of an atom bomb in 1949. The revelation

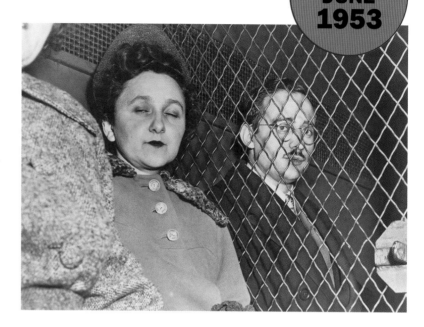

that the Soviet nuclear weapons programme had been helped by information provided by physicist Klaus Fuchs and other "atom spies"

Ethel and Julius Rosenberg could be seen as innocent victims or sinister villains.

"A clear and present danger"

"There exists a world Communist movement . . . whose purpose it is, by treachery, deceit, infiltration into other groups (governmental and otherwise), espionage, sabotage, terrorism, and any other means deemed necessary, to establish a Communist totalitarian dictatorship in countries throughout the world. . . . The Communist movement in the United States . . . presents a clear and present danger to the security of the United States and to the existence of free American institutions."

From the preamble to the 1950 U.S. Internal Security Act.

TIMELINE

**COUNTERING
"COMMUNIST
SUBVERSION"
1947–1954**

**September
1947**
▶ House Un-American
Activities Committee
(HUAC) investigates
Communist influence
in Hollywood.

**August 3,
1948**
▶ Whittaker Chambers
names alleged
Communist agents,
including State
Department official
Alger Hiss.

**August 29,
1949**
▶ The Soviet Union
tests its first atom
bomb.

**February 9,
1950**
▶ Senator McCarthy
claims to have names
of Communists
working for the U.S.
government.

**March 1,
1950**
▶ Scientist Klaus Fuchs
is jailed in Britain for
revealing atomic
secrets to the Soviet
Union.

**September
23, 1950**
▶ U.S. Internal Security
Act is passed, aiming
to crack down on
Communist
subversion.

**March 29,
1951**
▶ Julius and Ethel
Rosenberg are found
guilty of espionage.

**June 19,
1953**
▶ The Rosenbergs are
executed.

**December 2,
1954**
▶ U.S. Senate condemns
McCarthy.

*Senator Joe McCarthy
holds up alleged
evidence of Communist
subversion in the U.S.
Army in July 1954.*

opened the way for paranoia. In February 1950, an obscure senator, Joe McCarthy, won instant prominence by claiming to possess a list of Communist agents working inside the U.S. government. Over the following years, McCarthy became the self-appointed leader of a witch hunt to root out Communists in all areas of American life.

A STEP TOO FAR

McCarthyism partly flourished because the Soviet Union really was running spy networks in the U.S.—just as the American CIA was spying on the Soviet bloc. Julius Rosenberg almost certainly did pass secrets to the Soviets, although whether his wife was a spy is less clear. But eventually the U.S. tired of McCarthy. In 1954, his efforts to identify alleged Communists in the U.S. Army proved a step too far and he was condemned by the U.S. Senate. However, many aspects of the McCarthy period—for example, bans on some Hollywood scriptwriters—survived into the 1960s.

CROSS-REFERENCE
COLD WAR SPIES:
PAGES 22–23

Hungarian Uprising Suppressed

The uprising that took place in Hungary in 1956 was a graphic demonstration of the degree of popular discontent with Communist rule and Soviet domination in Eastern Europe. It also showed, though, how difficult it would be to achieve political change in the Soviet bloc in the context of the Cold War.

The background to the uprising was a limited liberalization of Communist rule in the Soviet Union after Stalin's death in March 1953. In the power struggle that followed, Nikita Khrushchev eventually emerged as Soviet leader. In February 1956, at a closed session of the Soviet Communist Party, Khrushchev denounced the excesses of Stalin's dictatorial rule. Khrushchev's policy of "destalinization," which included the release of many political prisoners, stimulated hopes of liberal reform in Eastern Europe.

POLISH PROTESTS

In June 1956, protests erupted in Poznan, Poland. They were motivated by the low standard of living, a desire for political freedom, and nationalist hostility to domination by the Soviet Union. Soviet troops suppressed the demonstrations but Khrushchev allowed a relatively liberal Polish Communist, Wladislaw Gomulka, to take control and institute a small

Soviet tanks roll through the deserted streets of the Hungarian capital, Budapest, in November 1956.

measure of reform. The events in Poland in turn stimulated protests in Hungary, where a popular movement developed calling for democracy and national independence.

SOVIETS ASSERT CONTROL

In October 1956, Imre Nagy, a pro-reform Communist, was appointed Hungarian prime minister. He announced the withdrawal of Hungary from the Soviet-led Warsaw Pact alliance. In response the Soviet Union sent in its army. Hungary called for the U.S. to come to its defense but the U.S. government refused. After heavy fighting, Soviet tanks took control of the Hungarian capital, Budapest. Nagy was arrested and eventually executed. However, as in Poland, Khrushchev also attempted to avoid future trouble by installing a relatively liberal Communist in power, Janos Kadar.

March 5, 1953 ▶ Death of Soviet dictator Joseph Stalin.

June 17, 1953 ▶ Soviet troops suppress workers' protests in East Berlin.

July 5, 1953 ▶ Imre Nagy becomes prime minister of Hungary in move toward liberalization of Communist regime.

April 18, 1955 ▶ Nagy is dismissed because of his relatively liberal policies.

February 25, 1956 ▶ Khrushchev attacks Stalin's policies in speech to Soviet Communist Party conference.

June 28, 1956 ▶ Polish Communist authorities fire on protesters in Poznan.

October 23, 1956 ▶ Hungarian protesters demand democracy; Nagy is reappointed prime minister.

October 31, 1956 ▶ Hungary withdraws from Warsaw Pact.

November 4, 1956 ▶ Soviet forces invade Hungary to suppress uprising.

June 16, 1958 ▶ Nagy is hanged after a secret trial.

The U.S.'s failure to support the Hungarian uprising showed that it was prepared to accept the continuance of Soviet control of Eastern Europe. Backing Eastern European attempts to overthrow Communism carried too high a risk of full-scale war. Without U.S. support, the peoples of Eastern Europe had no way of resisting Soviet military might.

CROSS-REFERENCE
SOVIET INVASION OF CZECHOSLOVAKIA: PAGES 30–31

Imre Nagy, the Hungarian Communist who became leader of the 1956 uprising.

Appeal to the world

"The whole world will see how the Russian armed forces, contrary to all treaties and conventions, are crushing the resistance of the Hungarian people . . . tomorrow, or the day after tomorrow, it will be the turn of other countries, because the imperialism of Moscow knows no borders and is only biding its time."

The last message of Hungarian Prime Minister Imre Nagy before his arrest. Quoted in Internet Modern History Sourcebook, www.fordham.edu

First Sputnik Launch

Sputnik 1, the first human-made Earth satellite, was an aluminium sphere weighing only 84kg (184 lb).

The launch of Sputnik 1, the first artificial satellite, by the Soviet Union in October 1957 was a sensational propaganda coup. It gave the Soviets and the Communist system immense prestige worldwide, allowing Soviet leader Khrushchev to claim that his country was overtaking the U.S. in economic and technological progress. The contest for prestige between the two superpowers was crucial in a world in which many newly independent former colonies were choosing between the capitalist and Communist ideologies and economic systems. The launch of Sputnik also had serious military implications. A Soviet rocket capable of launching a satellite into space could also carry a nuclear warhead to America. And satellites equipped with powerful cameras could be used to spy on enemy territory.

THE SPACE RACE UNFOLDS

Although the U.S. soon launched its own first satellite, the Soviet Union maintained a lead in space exploration into the early 1960s. When Yuri Gagarin became the first man to orbit the Earth in April 1961, the Americans felt a desperate need to fight back. President John F. Kennedy

Sense of shock

"In the Open West, you learn to live closely with the sky. . . . But now, somehow, in some new way, the **sky seemed almost alien.** I also remember the profound shock of realizing that it might be possible for another nation to achieve technological superiority over this great country."

U.S. President Lyndon B. Johnson's reaction to learning of Sputnik 1's launch before he became U.S. president in 1963. Quoted in Tom D. Crouch, *Aiming for the Stars* (Smithsonian Press, 1999).

CROSS-REFERENCE
U.S.–SOVIET
SPACE
COOPERATION:
PAGES 36–37

TIMELINE | THE SPACE RACE 1957–1969

October 4, 1957	Soviet Union launches its first satellite into orbit.
November 3, 1957	Laika, a dog, is sent into space on board Sputnik 2.
January 31, 1958	U.S. launches its first satellite, Explorer 1.
April 12, 1961	Soviet cosmonaut Yuri Gagarin is first man in space.
May 25, 1961	President Kennedy commits the U.S. to landing a man on the Moon before the end of the decade.
February 20, 1962	John Glenn becomes first American to orbit the Earth.
June 16, 1963	Soviet cosmonaut Valentina Tereshkova is first woman in space.
January 14, 1966	Sergei Korolev, mastermind of the Soviet space program, dies.
November 9, 1967	U.S. tests Saturn V rocket carrying lunar module.
July 20, 1969	U.S. astronauts land on the Moon.

announced a program to land a man on the Moon, if possible by the end of the decade. At the time few people thought that this could be done. The U.S., however, devoted massive resources to this goal.

THE SOVIETS FALL BEHIND

By the mid-1960s, the Soviet Union was failing to keep up with the pace of U.S. progress. The landing of U.S. astronauts on the Moon in July 1969 allowed the Americans to claim credibly to have won the space race.

The eventual success of the U.S. was ominous for the Soviet system, which had always claimed to be superior to capitalism at developing the economic and technological potential of human society. The U.S. was particularly successful at developing computers, which played a major part in the Moon landing. The failure of the Soviet Union to match Western technological progress proved crucial to the outcome of the Cold War.

U.S. astronaut Edwin "Buzz" Aldrin walks on the Moon in July 1969, photographed by mission commander Neil Armstrong.

U2 Spyplane Shot Down

The U2 was a high-flying reconnaissance aircraft used by the U.S. Central Intelligence Agency (CIA) for secret spy flights over the Soviet Union. In May 1960, a U2 piloted by Gary Powers was shot down by a Soviet missile. Powers survived and was paraded on television by the Soviets as proof that the spy flights were taking place. Soviet leader Khrushchev expressed outrage at the flights, using this as a pretext for walking out of a summit meeting with U.S. and British leaders in Paris. Powers returned to the U.S. in 1962, exchanged in a "spy swap" for Rudolf Abel, a KGB spy who had been arrested by the Americans.

A CLIMATE OF SUSPICION

Espionage was central to the Cold War. Both the CIA and its Soviet equivalent, the KGB, were large-scale organizations striving to uncover the other side's military secrets. One major form of espionage was the interception of communications, which then had to be decoded by codebreakers. Another involved the use of agents with access to secret documents. On both sides there were individuals prepared to betray information about their own country. For example, Soviet agents such as Anatoli Golitsyn and Oleg Penkovsky provided information for the West. On the other side, a group of well-educated Britons who had converted to Communism in the 1930s—including Anthony Blunt, Guy Burgess, Kim Philby, and Donald Maclean—deliberately found work in the British secret service or foreign office to spy for the Soviet Union. The revelation of their activities created a climate of suspicion in which anyone might be seen as an agent or a double agent. James Angleton, the CIA's chief counterespionage officer from the 1950s to the 1970s, even believed that a British prime minister, Harold Wilson, was a Soviet agent.

When the use of high-altitude spy planes was followed by the introduction of reconnaissance satellites in the 1960s, any point on Earth could be kept under more or less permanent surveillance. But the need for other forms of intelligence, including secret agents, did not disappear. Both the CIA and the KGB continued to fight their shadowy war up to the end of the Cold War.

Soviet leader Nikita Khrushchev shows the Soviet parliament a sheet of espionage photos taken by Gary Powers' U2 spyplane.

In 1955, surrounded by journalists, Kim Philby, standing, cheerfully denies being a Soviet spy. The truth emerged eight years later.

Reason for being a spy

"I left [Cambridge] university with a degree and with the conviction that my life must be **devoted to Communism.** I have long since lost my degree... But I have retained the conviction."

Kim Philby, from his autobiography *My Silent War* (Panther Books, 1969).

CROSS-REFERENCE
ROSENBERGS
EXECUTED FOR
SPYING: PAGES
16–17

Berlin Wall Erected

In August 1961, Berlin was the only place in which people could move freely across the "Iron Curtain" separating Eastern and Western Europe. It was possible to pass from Soviet-controlled East Berlin into West Berlin, controlled by Britain, the U.S., and France. From there, Easterners could move on to the rest of Western Europe. As a result, Communist-ruled East Germany suffered a constant drain of its population. By the summer of 1961, 30,000 East Germans were passing through West Berlin to new lives in West Germany every month. This population drain threatened East Germany with collapse.

KHRUSHCHEV THREATENS WAR

The crisis over Berlin occurred at a critical moment in the Cold War. The U.S. had a new president, John F. Kennedy. Soviet leader Khrushchev had adopted an aggressive stance, hoping to pressure the inexperienced Kennedy into concessions. At a summit meeting in Vienna in June 1961, Khrushchev threatened war if Western troops were not withdrawn from West Berlin within six months. Kennedy responded by committing the U.S. to fight if necessary to defend West Berlin. Measures were taken in the U.S. to prepare for a nuclear war, including building radiation-proof shelters.

Khrushchev did not go through with his threat to take over West Berlin. Instead, he gave the East German government the go-ahead to build a wall along the border between East and West Berlin, to stop Easterners leaving for the West. Construction of the Wall began on August 17, 1961. The U.S. and its allies made only token efforts to protest, privately

A builder cements part of the Wall dividing East and West Berlin under the watchful eye of East German border guards.

CROSS-REFERENCE
FALL OF THE
BERLIN WALL:
PAGES 44–45

TIMELINE	BERLIN CRISIS 1961–1963
January 20, 1961	John F. Kennedy takes office as president of the U.S.
June 4, 1961	At a meeting with Kennedy in Vienna, Khrushchev states determination to end existing situation in Berlin.
July 25, 1961	Kennedy says that the U.S. is ready to fight in defense of West Berlin.
July 31, 1961	More than 30,000 East Germans have crossed into West Berlin in previous month.
August 13, 1961	Border between East and West Berlin is closed by East German authorities.
August 17, 1961	Construction of Berlin Wall begins.
August 24, 1961	Gunter Litfin is first person killed fleeing from East to West Berlin.
October 27, 1961	U.S. and Soviet tanks face up to one another at Berlin checkpoint.
June 26, 1963	President Kennedy visits West Berlin.

accepting that the Wall offered a workable solution to a dangerous situation. For Berliners, the division of their city was a nightmare. Families and friends were separated. Over the following years, many people died trying to cross the Wall.

Although it enabled East Germany to survive, the Wall was a serious propaganda defeat for the Communist bloc. Western powers could point to this solid and oppressive structure and claim that they alone represented freedom.

President Kennedy makes his famous speech in West Berlin on June 26, 1963, five months before his assassination.

Kennedy on the Wall

"There are many people in the world who really don't understand . . . what is the great issue between the free world and the Communist world. Let them come to Berlin. There are some who say that communism is the wave of the future. Let them come to Berlin. . . . All free men, wherever they may live, are citizens of Berlin, and, therefore, as a free man, I take pride in the words: **Ich bin ein Berliner.**"

President J. F. Kennedy, speaking in West Berlin, June 26, 1963.

Kennedy Declares Naval Blockade of Cuba

The Cuban missile crisis of 1962 was the climax of the Cold War—the nearest the world has ever come to a full-scale nuclear war. The background to the crisis was the establishment in Cuba of a revolutionary government led by Fidel Castro. Castro's left-wing policies led to conflict with the U.S. and alliance with the Soviet Union. In April 1961, the U.S. backed an invasion of Cuba by anti-Castro Cuban exiles. The invasion failed but the U.S. was expected to try again.

Castro asked Soviet leader Khrushchev to provide forces to defend Cuba. Khrushchev saw an opportunity to alter the nuclear balance of power. The Soviet Union knew that the U.S. not only had far more long-range nuclear bombs and missiles but also had shorter-range missiles stationed close to the Soviet border in Turkey. By installing its own nuclear missiles in Cuba, the Soviet Union could defend the Cuban revolution and redress the nuclear balance.

Using photographs taken by a U2 spyplane the U.S. discovered that Soviet missile bases were being established in Cuba. After a week of intense debate within the U.S. leadership, on October 22, 1962, President Kennedy made a public statement revealing the existence of the missile bases and calling for the missiles' immediate withdrawal. He announced a naval blockade of Cuba to stop delivery of any further Soviet military supplies.

LAST-MINUTE SOLUTION

Fortunately both Kennedy and Khrushchev wanted to avoid a nuclear war. The two sides came perilously close to conflict at sea, and one U.S. aircraft was shot down over Cuba but in private a face-saving solution was found. The Soviet Union would withdraw its missiles from Cuba; the U.S. would promise not to invade Cuba and would withdraw its missiles from Turkey.

President Kennedy signs the order establishing a naval blockade of Cuba. There was a risk the blockade could lead to nuclear war.

Against war

"It seems likely that within a week you will be dead to please American madmen. . . . I urge every human being who loves life to come out in the streets of our country and demonstrate our demand to live and let live. **There must not be WAR.**"

Press release by British philosopher and peace campaigner Bertrand Russell. Like many left-wingers, Russell blamed the U.S. for the missile crisis, ignoring Soviet aggression. Quoted in Ray Monk, *Bertrand Russell* (Jonathan Cape, 2000).

After the missile crisis, a "hot line" was set up for emergency communication between the White House and the Kremlin. Kennedy won widespread praise for his handling of the crisis but he was assassinated 13 months later. Khrushchev was harshly criticized within the Soviet leadership for having taken such risks. He was forced out of power by his colleagues in 1964.

CROSS-REFERENCE
THE CARIBBEAN IN THE COLD WAR: PAGES 34–35
DÉTENTE: PAGES 36–37

Bearded Cuban leader Fidel Castro and Soviet premier Nikita Khrushchev meet at the United Nations in September 1960.

U.S. Marines Sent into Vietnam

In March 1965, U.S. President Lyndon B. Johnson committed U.S. ground forces to a war that was being fought in the former French colony of Vietnam. A Communist-led Vietnamese guerrilla movement had driven the French out in 1954, establishing a Communist state in the northern half of the country. In South Vietnam, however, the U.S. had backed the anticommunist regime of Ngo Dinh Diem.

INCREASING U.S. INVOLVEMENT

From 1959, the North Vietnamese government promoted a guerrilla war against Diem's regime, seeking to unify Vietnam under Communist rule. The U.S. sent in military advisers to help Diem fight the war. However, Diem's regime was corrupt and unpopular. In November 1963, the U.S. backed a coup by South Vietnamese officers in the course of which Diem was assassinated. U.S. military involvement escalated as Communist guerrillas took over ever-larger areas of South Vietnam.

Although from 1965 U.S. armed forces were sent in on a massive scale to fight the guerrillas in the South Vietnamese paddy fields and jungles, the Americans did not invade North Vietnam, because it was believed this might bring China or the Soviet Union into the war. However, the U.S. did carry out a bombing campaign against the North, hoping that air attacks would persuade the North Vietnamese to call off the war in the

U.S. soldiers patrol the South Vietnamese countryside. At the peak of the war, over half a million Americans were serving in Vietnam.

Escalating U.S. commitment to Vietnam, 1965–1969					
	1965	1966	1967	1968	1969
Troop levels	184,300	385,300	485,600	536,100	543,482
Combat deaths	1,369	5,008	9,378	14,592	9,414

In total, more than 2.5 million Americans served in Vietnam between 1964 and 1973, of whom 58,336 died. Sixty-one percent of those killed were aged 21 or under.

TIMELINE	THE VIETNAM CONFLICT 1954–1975
August 1954	▶ Vietnam gains independence from France, with the North ruled by the Communists and the South eventually by Ngo Dinh Diem.
1959	▶ Communist-led guerrilla war begins in South Vietnam.
November 1961	▶ U.S. sends military advisers to aid South Vietnam.
November 2, 1963	▶ Diem is assassinated in a military coup.
August 2–4, 1964	▶ Gulf of Tonkin incident leads to first U.S. bombing of North Vietnam.
March 8, 1965	▶ U.S. Marines are sent to South Vietnam.
January– February 1968	▶ Communist forces attack South Vietnamese cities in Tet Offensive.
October 31, 1968	▶ U.S. bombing of North Vietnam is halted to allow peace talks to begin.
January 27, 1973	▶ Peace accords signed, allowing final withdrawal of U.S. forces from Vietnam.
April 30, 1975	▶ North Vietnam defeats the South and wins the war.

South. All the bombing achieved was to stimulate an antiwar movement in the U.S.

WITHDRAWAL OF U.S. TROOPS

With a strong will to fight and sufficient arms supplies, mostly from the Soviet Union, the Vietnamese Communists inflicted heavy casualties on the Americans. By 1968, with no end to the war in sight, American public opinion turned strongly in favor of "bringing the boys back home." After lengthy peace talks, the withdrawal of U.S. troops was completed in January 1973. In theory, U.S. forces were supposed to return to defend South Vietnam if the war resumed but when the North Vietnamese army overran the South in 1975, the U.S. did nothing in response.

Vietnam and the neighboring states of Cambodia and Laos all came under Communist rule in a devastating setback for U.S. foreign policy. The cost of the conflict to the Vietnamese people was huge, with millions dead and much of the land devastated by bombing or poisoned by the use of chemical warfare agents.

CROSS-REFERENCE KOREAN WAR: PAGES 12–13 CHINA–U.S. RELATIONS: PAGES 32–33

Protesters march through Washington, D.C. in 1969, calling for an end to the war in Vietnam. Some carry Vietnamese Communist flags.

Soviet Invasion Ends Prague Spring

In Prague, a young Czech climbs on top of a Soviet tank during the protests that followed the Soviet invasion of August 1968.

Early in 1968, a liberal Communist, Alexander Dubcek, became head of the ruling Communist Party in Czechoslovakia. Like Mikhail Gorbachev in the Soviet Union two decades later, Dubcek was convinced that freedom of the individual, democracy, and economic prosperity could flourish in a Communist state. In April, Dubcek announced a programme of liberal reforms, designed to create "communism with a human face." This unleashed a wave of political activism and free expression in Czechoslovakia, especially in the capital, Prague. As the "Prague Spring" gathered momentum, Dubcek found it difficult to set a limit to the reforms he had initiated.

At this time, the Soviet Union was under the leadership of Leonid Brezhnev, a cautious bureaucrat solidly opposed to any change in the established Communist system in the Soviet bloc. Brezhnev and his colleagues regarded the reform movement in Czechoslovakia with deep suspicion. At the start of August, in a tough meeting with the Soviet leader, Dubcek promised that Czechoslovakia would remain a Communist-ruled state loyal to the Warsaw Pact alliance. But the Soviet Union doubted Dubcek could really keep the lid on pressure for more radical change from the Czechoslovak people.

SOVIET-IMPOSED CRACKDOWN

On August 20, Soviet and other Warsaw Pact forces invaded Czechoslovakia. Unlike in Hungary in 1956, there was no armed resistance but Czechs massed in the streets to demonstrate their hostility to the Soviet tank crews occupying Prague. The Soviets bullied Dubcek into reversing his reforms and he was later forced to resign. Hardline

Communism was reimposed in Czechoslovakia. People who refused to toe the line were thrown out of their jobs. Thousands fled into exile. Opposition to the Soviet-imposed crackdown was dramatized by the public suicide of student Jan Palach in Prague in 1969. But the Czechoslovak population was powerless to change the government imposed on it. Brezhnev justified the invasion by claiming the right to uphold Communist rule anywhere in the Soviet bloc by force if necessary. Known as the Brezhnev Doctrine, this view was in practice accepted by the U.S., which made no effort to intervene in the crisis.

CROSS-REFERENCE
GORBACHEV'S REFORMS: PAGES 42–43
COMMUNISM FALLS: PAGES 44–45

Leonid Brezhnev, front left, stands alongside Alexander Dubcek as a Communist colleague, before the events of 1968.

The Brezhnev Doctrine

"The weakening of any of the links in the world system of socialism directly affects all the socialist countries. . . . Discharging their internationalist duty toward the fraternal peoples of Czechoslovakia and defending their own socialist gains, the Soviet Union and the other **socialist states had to act decisively** . . . against the anti-socialist forces in Czechoslovakia."

Brezhnev justifies the invasion of Czechoslovakia in a speech in November 1968. Quoted in Internet Modern History Sourcebook, www.fordham.edu

Nixon Visits China

Two of the world's most powerful men meet: Chairman Mao Zedong and President Richard Nixon in Beijing, February 1972.

For more than two decades after Communist rule was established in mainland China, the U.S. continued to insist that the Chinese Nationalists, ruling the island of Taiwan, were China's true government. Thus the visit of President Richard Nixon to Communist China in February 1972 marked a startling reversal of U.S. policy. Images of Nixon conversing with Chinese leader Mao Zedong told the world that a major shift in international relations was under way.

COMMUNIST SPLIT

At the start of the Cold War, the U.S. had assumed that all Communist-ruled states constituted a single unified bloc opposed to the U.S.-led "free world." Communists, for their part, also tended to see themselves as involved in a single worldwide revolutionary struggle. In 1960, however, the alliance between the Soviet Union and China, the world's two largest Communist states, broke apart. The Chinese Communists denounced the Soviets for allegedly abandoning the true path of the revolution. The Soviets responded by withdrawing all aid and personnel from China. Relations between the two countries had deteriorated to the point of open border warfare by 1969.

Mao meets Nixon

"Mao Zedong summoned the leader of the free world to an audience at one hour's notice. . . . Mao greeted Nixon, Kissinger, and me in a small, simple dwelling; surrounded by books, not courtiers; **looking and sounding like the coarse peasant he was.** He conducted the conversation in seemingly casual fashion, moving with broad brush strokes . . . from one topic to another. Taiwan was a small problem. Russia was a big problem. . . . When the 65 minutes were up, the already frail Mao had sketched China's strategic positions on all major issues."

U.S. diplomat Winston Lord describes the first Nixon–Mao meeting, *Time* magazine, September 27, 1999.

TACTICAL ALLIANCE

After Nixon became U.S. president in 1969, he appointed Henry Kissinger as his national security adviser. Kissinger saw that an alliance between the U.S. and China would weaken the position of the Soviet Union. The Chinese were only too willing to gain closer links with the Americans, judging that this would strengthen their own position relative to the Soviets. Nixon's visit to China had few practical effects—the U.S. continued officially to recognize the government of Taiwan as China's government until 1979. But it showed that a Communist state was no longer necessarily an enemy of the U.S.

Subsequent events, including a border war between Vietnam and China in 1979, would underline divisions between Communist countries. The Chinese later went on to show, even more surprisingly, that a Communist-ruled state could successfully adopt a capitalist economy.

Soviet soldiers keep watch on the border with China after clashes between forces of the two Communist giants in 1969.

CROSS-REFERENCE NIXON'S POLICY TOWARD SOVIET UNION: PAGES 36–37

U.S.-backed Coup in Chile

On September 11, 1973, the government of Chile was overthrown in a military coup. Chile's democratically elected president, Salvatore Allende, died during fighting at the presidential palace. The coup installed a military dictator, General Augusto Pinochet, in power. Thousands of Allende's supporters were arrested; many were tortured and some killed. Although the U.S. was in principle devoted to freedom and democracy, it approved of the coup and gave the Pinochet government its full support. This was because Allende, although democratically elected, was a Communist.

U.S. POLICY IN THE AMERICAS

The determination of the U.S. to keep Communism out of Latin America and the Caribbean, whether local people wanted it or not, led it to support dictatorships and military governments in many countries, including Brazil and Argentina. The example of Fidel Castro's Cuba was always present in the minds of U.S. leaders. Castro had overthrown a U.S.-backed dictatorship in 1959 with widespread popular support and then led Cuba into an alliance with the Soviet Union. Castro's colleague Ernesto "Che" Guevara had set out to encourage anti-U.S. uprisings throughout Latin America, before he was killed in 1967. U.S. governments were determined that no other pro-Soviet state would emerge in the Americas and were prepared to use any methods needed to stop it.

Direct U.S. military intervention and U.S. support for anticommunist dictators did succeed in largely excluding Soviet influence from extending beyond Cuba. The only subsequent major setback for U.S. Cold War policy in the Americas was the overthrow of a U.S.-backed dictatorship in Nicaragua by the Sandinistas in 1979. However, in the 1980s, the Sandinista regime was undermined by U.S. support for a destructive guerrilla war waged by Nicaraguan exiles.

COLD WAR IN THE DEVELOPING WORLD

The situation in Latin America and the Caribbean was typical of all the developing world—or "Third World"—during the Cold War period.

General Pinochet, center, and military colleagues take control after carrying out a coup in Chile in 1973.

34

Kissinger's view

"I don't see why we need to stand by and **watch a country go Communist** due to the irresponsibility of its own people. The issues are much too important for the Chilean voters to be left to decide for themselves."

U.S. Secretary of State Henry Kissinger, National Security Council meeting, June 27, 1970.

This Cuban soldier, right, was sent by Fidel Castro to fight on behalf of the left-wing government of Ethiopia in a war in East Africa.

Problems of poverty and inequality tended to create popular support for left-wing governments or movements that promised economic progress and a fairer sharing of wealth. The U.S. would oppose these as pro-Communist, while the Soviet Union and its Cuban allies offered them support in the hope of extending Communist influence. This happened in African countries such as Angola, Mozambique, Ethiopia, and Congo, as well as in the Americas. Becoming part of the Cold War battlefield was almost always disastrous for local people wherever they were.

CROSS-REFERENCE CASTRO: PAGES 26–27 SOVIETS INVADE AFGHANISTAN: PAGES 38–39

Apollo–Soyuz Mission

On July 17, 1975, Soviet cosmonauts aboard a Soyuz spacecraft and U.S. astronauts aboard an Apollo vehicle met in space. They exchanged gifts and words of friendship, worked side by side for two days, and then returned to Earth. Conducted amid a blaze of publicity, it was the first joint space mission staged by the two superpowers.

Since the space race between the U.S. and the Soviet Union had been a high-profile expression of Cold War rivalry, the joint mission was an effective symbol of cooperation and good will between the two sides.

THE POLICY OF DÉTENTE

For a decade from the late 1960s, Soviet leader Leonid Brezhnev and a succession of U.S. presidents— Richard Nixon, Gerald Ford, and Jimmy Carter—pursued a policy of détente. Its most practical expression was a search for agreement on a halt to the nuclear arms race. By the end of the 1960s, each side had sufficient nuclear weapons to destroy the other many times over, so it made sense to halt the expansion of nuclear arsenals. The Strategic Arms Limitation Talks (SALT) took three years to achieve a first agreement in 1972. Further progress was painfully slow, however. The following seven years were spent negotiating SALT II—a treaty that was never ratified by the U.S. Congress.

In truth, despite gestures such as the Apollo–Soyuz mission and the Soviet Union signing the 1975 Helsinki Accords guaranteeing human rights, the Cold War was far from over.

The members of the joint Apollo–Soyuz mission pose together, U.S. astronauts in orange, Soviet cosmonauts in green.

Superpower nuclear arsenals in 1979

	Intercontinental ballistic missiles (ICBMs)		Submarine-launched ballistic missiles (SLBMs)		Long-range bombers
	missiles	warheads	missiles	warheads	
U.S.	1,054	2,154	656	5,440	431
Soviet Union	1,398	4,726	1,028	1,488	156

The two superpowers continued to back opposite sides in conflicts around the world. In 1973, for example, Soviet-armed Egypt and Syria fought U.S.-armed Israel in the Middle East. In 1975, the U.S. promoted wars against left-wing regimes in Angola and Mozambique, prompting Cuba to send troops to Angola to defend them.

Nixon, left, and Brezhnev, right, meet for talks in Moscow in July 1974. The following month the Watergate scandal forced Nixon to resign.

THE END OF DÉTENTE

In general, the NATO alliance became nervous that the SALT process had given the Soviet Union a strategic advantage. In November 1979, NATO decided to station U.S. Cruise missiles in Europe, hoping to pressure the Soviets into concessions at the arms talks. The following month, the Soviet invasion of Afghanistan ended the period of détente.

COLD WAR IN THE DEVELOPING WORLD: PAGES 34–35
ARMS CUTS: PAGES 42–43

Soviet Invasion of Afghanistan

24 DECEMBER 1979

In December 1979, the Soviet Union sent large-scale military forces across its southern border into Afghanistan. They were sent to defend a Communist regime threatened by Afghan mujahidin guerrilla fighters. The invasion was denounced by Western leaders as a blatant act of aggression, ending the period of détente between the U.S. and the Soviet Union.

Afghanistan had been a monarchy until 1973, when a coup brought a left-wing government to power. In April 1978, Afghan Communists seized control and set in motion a drive to transform the country. This stirred up armed resistance among the tribes of rural Afghanistan, who resented interference in their traditional way of life. The Communist government called in Soviet military advisers to help fight the mujahidin who, from the summer of 1979, had the backing of the American CIA. As the war went badly for the Communist side, the Soviets decided to send in their army in force.

A VICIOUS WAR

The Soviet Union blamed the head of the Afghan government, Hafizullah Amin, for the deteriorating situation. At the same time as sending in troops, they assassinated Amin and replaced him with another Afghan Communist, Babrak Karmal. However, Karmal was no more capable of winning the support of the Afghan people than his predecessor.

Soviets' Vietnam

"The day that the Soviets officially crossed the border, I wrote to President Carter: "We now have the opportunity of giving to the Soviet Union its Vietnam War." Indeed, **for almost 10 years,** Moscow had to carry on a war . . . that brought about the demoralization and finally the breakup of the Soviet empire."

Zbigniew Brzezinski, adviser to U.S. President Jimmy Carter. Quoted in *Le Nouvel Observateur*, January 1998.

Soviet armored vehicles and trucks arrive in Kabul as the Soviet Union builds up its military presence in January 1980.

TIMELINE	**SOVIET INFLUENCE IN AFGHANISTAN 1973–1992**
1973	▶ Daoud Khan takes power in Afghanistan in a coup backed by Communist Parcham.
April 27, 1978	▶ Afghan Communists assassinate Daoud and seize power; Soviet advisers are invited into Afghanistan.
July 1979	▶ The U.S. provides backing for a revolt by mujahidin fighters against the Afghan government.
December 24, 1979	▶ Soviets invade Afghanistan and install Babrak Karmal in power.
July–August 1980	▶ Olympic Games in Moscow. Sixty-five countries, including U.S., refuse to participate in protest over Afghanistan.
September 1986	▶ U.S. begins supplying Stinger ground-to-air missiles to Afghan mujahidin.
May–February 1988	▶ Soviet troops withdraw from Afghanistan.
April 1992	▶ Afghanistan becomes an Islamic state after mujahidin capture Kabul.

Armed and financed not only by the Americans but also by Pakistan, Saudi Arabia, and China, the mujahidin restricted the Soviet forces to control of towns.

With the backing of the U.S., Afghan mujahidin guerrillas organize to fight against the Soviet army.

Fought with great viciousness on both sides, the war caused heavy casualties. In nine years, roughly one million Afghanis and at least 15,000 Soviet soldiers were killed.

SOVIET WITHDRAWAL

The Afghan war was unpopular in the Soviet Union, particularly causing unrest in Muslim areas of the country. When the U.S. began supplying the mujahidin with Stinger missiles, which allowed ground fighters to shoot down Soviet helicopters, the faint chance of the Soviet Union winning the war faded. Mikhail Gorbachev, Soviet leader from 1985, sought a face-saving path to withdrawal from Afghanistan. The last Soviet forces left in 1989. The mujahidin took over Afghanistan three years later.

CROSS-REFERENCE
VIETNAM WAR:
PAGES 28–29
GORBACHEV
REFORMS SOVIET
UNION: PAGES
42–43

Polish Workers Occupy Gdansk Shipyard

On August 14, 1980, striking Polish workers occupied the shipyards in the port of Gdansk. Led by a blunt-spoken electrician, Lech Walesa, they insisted they would not leave until Poland's Communist government recognized their right to found a labor union independent of Communist control. The authorities caved in and recognized the independent labor union, Solidarity, on August 31. Solidarity became much more than a labor union—it was a movement for freedom and Polish national renewal.

POLISH REJECTION OF COMMUNISM

Poland had always been a difficult country for the Communists to rule. Poles were intensely nationalistic and detested domination by the Soviet Union. They were also mostly Catholics, rejecting the atheist ideology of Communism. The election of a Polish pope, John Paul II, in 1978 excited Catholic sentiment and national pride. When the pope visited Poland in 1979, Poles gathered in their millions to hear him speak. It was a mass demonstration of their allegiance to a belief opposed to Communism.

In the summer of 1980, the Polish government announced price rises in response to a worsening economic situation in the country. This provoked riots, strikes, and

Solidarity leader Lech Walesa is carried on the shoulders of colleagues during the strike at the Gdansk shipyards in 1980.

Strength through Solidarity

"The sole and basic source of our strength is the solidarity of . . . the nation, the solidarity of people who seek to live in dignity, truth, and in harmony with their conscience. . . . We shall not yield to violence. We shall not be deprived of union freedoms. We shall never agree with sending people to prison for their convictions. . . . The defense of our rights and our dignity, as well as efforts never to let ourselves be overcome by the feeling of hatred—**this is the road we have chosen.**"

Lech Walesa's Nobel prize lecture, 1983.

demonstrations, climaxing in the occupation of the shipyards. Once Solidarity was legalized, the Communist regime had lost the moral authority to rule Poland. But the Solidarity movement carefully avoided challenging the Communist Party's formal hold on power at governmental level, because they feared the Soviet Union would send in its tanks to save the regime.

IMPOSITION OF MARTIAL LAW

The Soviet Union did not intervene, however. Instead, at the end of 1981, the head of the Polish army, General Jaruzelski, took over the government, imposed martial law, and arrested Solidarity leaders. The crackdown on Solidarity gave fuel to supporters of U.S. president Ronald Reagan and British prime minister Margaret Thatcher, who were denouncing the horrors of Communism.

The imposition of rule by the army revealed the economic and political bankruptcy of the Polish Communist Party, which had failed to win popular support after 34 years in power.

FALL OF COMMUNISM IN EASTERN EUROPE: PAGES 44–45

Hundreds of thousands of Poles gather in the city of Krakow to see Pope John Paul II during his visit to Poland in 1979.

Reagan and Gorbachev Agree Arms Cuts

8 DECEMBER 1987

On December 8, 1987, at the end of a three-day summit meeting between U.S. president Ronald Reagan and Soviet leader Mikhail Gorbachev in Washington D.C., the U.S. and the Soviet Union signed the first agreement to reduce, rather than limit, nuclear arms. In the Intermediate Nuclear Forces treaty, the two sides agreed to get rid of all their medium-range nuclear missiles in Europe. In total, 1,752 Soviet and 859 U.S. missiles were to be dismantled in three years.

The agreement marked an astonishing turnaround from the early 1980s, when the Cold War had reached an intensity not seen since the time of the Cuban missile crisis. Taking office in 1980, Reagan was aggressively anticommunist, denouncing the Soviet Union as "the evil empire." His hardline stance was backed up by Margaret Thatcher, British prime minister from 1979, whom the Soviets named "the Iron Lady."

The stationing of U.S. Cruise missiles in European countries, including Britain, provoked widespread protests from opponents of nuclear weapons, such as the Campaign for Nuclear Disarmament (CND). There were also concerns that President Reagan's program for a space-based "Star Wars" defense system to protect the U.S. from missile attack would upset the balance of nuclear deterrence. The aggressive tone adopted by Western leaders made the Soviet Union seriously fear a surprise nuclear strike.

Mikhail Gorbachev and Ronald Reagan cheerfully sign the INF treaty at the Washington summit meeting in December 1987.

NEW LEADER, NEW ERA

However, a sharp change of direction followed the emergence of Gorbachev as Soviet leader in 1985. Gorbachev was keenly aware of serious problems in the Soviet bloc. The economies of Communist-ruled states, including the Soviet Union, had been performing badly for decades. The Soviets had been slipping ever farther behind the West in technological development. Gorbachev was convinced that only radical change could save the Communist system. He proposed to liberalize the Soviet political and economic system.

No more use of force

"Today we have entered an era when progress will be **based on the interests of all mankind. . . .** It is evident that force and the threat of force can no longer be, and should not be, instruments of foreign policy."

Mikhail Gorbachev's address to the United Nations, December 7, 1988.

Simultaneously, he wanted to end the Cold War with the West, partly because the cost of the nuclear arms race was crippling the Soviet economy.

Although suspicious, the U.S. government came guardedly to accept the genuineness of Gorbachev's desire for a new relationship based on trust and cooperation. In retrospect, the signing of the INF treaty can be seen as marking the effective end of the Cold War.

CROSS-REFERENCE
FALL OF SOVIET
COMMUNISM:
PAGES 44–45

The Campaign for Nuclear Disarmament (CND) protested at the stationing of U.S. Cruise missiles in Britain.

Fall of Berlin Wall

On the night of November 9–10, 1989, gates in the fortified Wall that had divided Berlin in two for 18 years were opened by their Communist guards. East Germans were suddenly free to walk through to the West. A wave of celebration spread through the city that was to last for several days and nights. The Cold War division of Europe was finally coming to an end.

The fate of Communist rule in Eastern Europe was always dependent on developments in Moscow. By 1989, Mikhail Gorbachev's drive to introduce democracy and economic liberalization in the Soviet Union was in full swing. The Soviet leadership encouraged the Communist regimes in Eastern Europe to follow a similar course of reform. When asked how far such reforms might go, Gorbachev and his colleagues made it plain that the Soviet Union would no longer intervene militarily to keep Communist parties in power.

THE COLLAPSE OF COMMUNISM

Hungary was the first East European country to embrace liberalization. As it shifted toward multi-party democracy, it partially opened its border to the West. Soon, tens of thousands of East German emigrants were flooding through Hungary to West Germany. Through the summer of 1989, while the East German government struggled hopelessly to maintain hardline Communist policies, a pro-democracy protest movement gathered strength. Meanwhile, a landslide victory for Solidarity in elections in Poland demonstrated once more the lack of popular support for Communist rule in Eastern Europe.

Celebrating Germans climb on top of the Berlin Wall in November 1989.

The Sinatra Doctrine

"We now have the Frank Sinatra doctrine. He has a song, "I Did It My Way." So every country decides on its own which road to take. . . . Political structures must be decided by the people who live there."

Soviet Foreign Ministry spokesman Gennadi Gerasimov, October 25, 1989, announces the end of the "Brezhnev Doctrine," accepting the freedom of East European countries to choose their own government.

The eventual collapse of East European Communism was spectacularly rapid. East Germany's hardline leader Erich Honecker resigned on October 18. Committed to liberalization, his Communist successors could see no alternative to opening the Wall. Within a month of this, East Germany's last Communist government resigned. During December, mass protests brought about the fall of Czechoslovakia's Communist regime. Only in Romania did the overthrow of Communism involve serious bloodshed.

Despite the fall of Communism in Eastern Europe, the Soviet Union was generally expected to survive as some form of Communist state. Yet Gorbachev's measures to introduce free speech and democracy unleashed a torrent of criticism of the regime, especially as the economy was in steep decline. At the end of 1991 the Soviet Union disintegrated.

Pro-democracy demonstrators throughout Eastern Europe helped drive Communist governments out of power.

Key Figures in the Cold War

LEONID BREZHNEV (1906–1982)

Brezhnev was appointed secretary-general of the Soviet Communist Party after the fall from power of Nikita Khrushchev in 1964. He also adopted the post of state president in 1977. Brezhnev pursued détente with the West, while simultaneously building up the strength of Soviet nuclear forces, upholding Communist rule in Eastern Europe and extending Soviet influence in Africa and Asia. Years of stagnation under his bureaucratic rule left the Soviet system in desperate need of reform.

ALEXANDER DUBCEK (1921–1992)

As first secretary of the Czechoslovak Communist Party from January 1968, Dubcek introduced wide-ranging political and economic reforms. He was driven from power eight months after the Soviet invasion of Czechoslovakia in August 1968. After the overthrow of the Communist regime in 1989, he was elected chairman of the Czechoslovak Federal Assembly.

MIKHAIL GORBACHEV (1931–)

Gorbachev became general secretary of the Soviet Communist Party in March 1985. He embarked on a bold program to reform the Soviet Communist system under the watchwords "glasnost" (openness) and "perestroika" (restructuring). He sought to end the Cold War, pursuing nuclear disarmament and withdrawing Soviet forces from Afghanistan. He was elected president of the Soviet Union in 1990 but the following year the Soviet state disintegrated, leaving Gorbachev without a country to lead.

JOHN F. KENNEDY (1917–1963)

Kennedy narrowly defeated Richard Nixon in the 1960 U.S. presidential elections. He adopted a tough anticommunist line early in his presidency, making it clear to the Soviets that he would go to war if necessary to defend West Berlin. But during the 1962 Cuban missile crisis he achieved a Soviet withdrawal while rejecting aggressive options that might have led to a nuclear conflict. Kennedy was assassinated in Dallas, Texas, in November 1963.

NIKITA KHRUSHCHEV (1894–1971)

Khrushchev became first secretary of the Soviet Communist Party after Stalin's death in 1953. In 1956, he denounced Stalin at a Communist Party congress. Khrushchev was a flamboyant personality who drew maximum propaganda advantage from the Soviet space program. His decision to base nuclear missiles in Cuba in 1962 brought the world close to nuclear war. In 1964, Khrushchev was forced out of power by more conservative Soviet colleagues.

HENRY KISSINGER (1923–)

German-born Henry Kissinger was chosen by President Nixon as his adviser on national security in 1969. He promoted a complex foreign policy combining the ruthless pursuit of U.S. national interests with a search for an improved relationship with China and the Soviet Union. He became U.S. Secretary of State in 1973, a post he continued to hold under Nixon's successor, President Ford.

JOSEPH McCARTHY (1909–1957)

In 1950, Senator Joe McCarthy became self-appointed leader of a witch hunt to expose Communist Party members and Soviet spies in various areas of American life. He employed an aggressive style of public interrogation, blackening the names of many innocent people. In 1954, he was condemned by the Senate and his influence collapsed. He died of alcoholism in 1957.

RONALD REAGAN (1911–2004)

Former movie actor Ronald Reagan was elected U.S. president in 1980. He took a tough line with the Soviet Union, which he denounced as the "evil empire." He backed Contra guerrillas against a left-wing government in Nicaragua and set in motion the "Star Wars" initiative for a space-based defense of the U.S. against nuclear missiles. But Reagan responded positively to Gorbachev's proposals for a dismantling of the Cold War.

JOSEPH STALIN (1879–1953)

Joseph Stalin caused the deaths of tens of millions of Soviet citizens in prison camps and purges 1930–1953. After the Soviet victory over Germany in 1945, his brutal rule was extended to Eastern Europe. Suspicious and cunning, Stalin always regarded his wartime alliance with the Western powers as only temporary. Although ready to pressure the U.S. through the Berlin blockade and backing North Korea in the Korean War, however, he was careful to avoid provoking a new world war.

HARRY S. TRUMAN (1884–1972)

Missouri senator Harry S. Truman became U.S. vice-president in 1944 and inherited the presidency when Roosevelt died in April 1945. He was, from the start, more suspicious of Soviet ambitions than Roosevelt had been, and in 1947 committed the U.S. to resisting the spread of Communism worldwide (the "Truman Doctrine"). He committed U.S. forces to the defense of South Korea in June 1950 and subsequently authorized a massive expansion in U.S. armed forces and nuclear weaponry.

LECH WALESA (1943–)

An electrician at the Lenin Shipyards in Gdansk, Poland, Walesa founded the Solidarity labor union in 1980 and led a movement of popular protest against the Communist government. When Solidarity was outlawed in December 1981, Walesa was arrested, although he was released a year later. He was awarded the Nobel Peace Prize in 1983. After the collapse of Communist rule in Eastern Europe, Walesa was elected president of Poland in December 1990.

Glossary

capitalism economic system based on private ownership of business

colonies countries occupied and ruled by a foreign power

Communism political and economic system involving rule by a single party and the control of industry and agriculture by the state

Communist subversion the attempt by Communists to overthrow or undermine non-Communist countries, using guerilla war or other non-democratic means

defect abandon one country to live in another, often rival, country

détente improved relations between hostile countries

Eastern Europe term used for Communist-ruled European countries east of the "Iron Curtain"

espionage spying or the use of spies to uncover secret information about the plans and activities of a foreign government

guerrillas soldiers who are not part of a regular army, who fight using ambushes and hit-and-run attacks

imperialism exercise of one state's political, military, or economic power over other countries

Iron Curtain term first used by Winston Churchill in 1946 to describe the fortified line dividing Communist Eastern Europe from Western Europe during the Cold War

liberalize make less strict

martial law rule by the army

mujahidin Islamic guerrilla fighters, especially in Afghanistan

NATO short for North Atlantic Treaty Organization; military alliance of the U.S. and West European countries opposed to the Soviet Union

propaganda ideas, information, or rumor that is spread with the intention of influencing public opinion

socialist term used by Communist regimes for their own economic and social system

Soviet bloc the Soviet Union and the countries of Eastern Europe

Soviet Union Communist state set up to replace the Russian Empire after the revolution of 1917; full name is the Union of Soviet Socialist Republics (USSR)

uprising rebellion

Western Allies the U.S., Britain, and their allies (cooperative partners) in Western Europe

Western Europe term used for European countries west of the Iron Curtain

Further Information

BOOKS

GENERAL OVERVIEW

Bryan Jones, Carol. *The Cold War* (*Teach Yourself History* series). Hodder Education, 2004.

McMahon, Robert J. *The Cold War* (*A Very Short Introduction* series). Oxford University Press, 2003.

SPECIFIC TOPICS

Cadbury, Deborah. *The Space Race.* HarperPerennial, 2006.

Grant, R. G. *The Berlin Wall.* Wayland, 1998.

Grant, R. G. *The Korean War.* Franklin Watts, 2004.

Philby, Kim. *My Silent War: Autobiography of a Spy.* Arrow, 2003.

DVDs

The Space Race—excellent BBC TV series

Thirteen Days—movie dramatization of the Cuban missile crisis, directed by Roger Donaldson and starring Kevin Costner (2001)

Dr Strangelove—humorous movie about nuclear deterrence, directed by Stanley Kubrick and starring Peter Sellers (1964)

WEBSITES

GENERAL COVERAGE

www.spartacus.schoolnet.co.uk/ColdWar.htm

http://edition.cnn.com/SPECIALS/cold.war/

Provides a good overview of the Cold War

SPECIFIC TOPICS

www.americanrhetoric.com/speeches

Full text and audio file of "Truman doctrine" speech

korea50.army.mil

A U.S.-Army view of the Korean War

www.eisenhower.archives.gov/dl/U2Incident/u2documents.html

Information on U2 spyplane and spying equipment

www.cubacrisis.net

Covers the Cuban missile crisis

www.berlin-wall.net

Information on the rise and fall of the Berlin Wall

www.nuclearweaponarchive.org/

Covers nuclear weaponry

PLACES TO VISIT

Imperial War Museum, London and Duxford, UK

Diefenbunker, Ontario, Canada—a four-storey nuclear bunker buried in a hillside

Hack Green nuclear bunker, Cheshire, UK

Index

Numbers in **bold** refer to photographs.